CONTENTS

WHO WERE THE VIKINGS?

A thousand years ago, a people called the Vikings lived in **Scandinavia**. The weather was cool and the soil was poor, so the Vikings sometimes found it hard to grow enough food. They kept sheep, hunted reindeer and caught fish, whales and **walrus**.

Some Vikings travelled to Russia and other parts of Europe, buying and selling goods. When times were hard they sailed to other lands, such as Britain, France and Iceland, where they built new homes.

VIKING SHIPS AND SAILORS

Viking ships were made of wood and were very sturdy. They had benches where up to 40 men could sit and row. They also had large, square sails, made of different-coloured strips of cloth. These gave the sails a striped appearance.

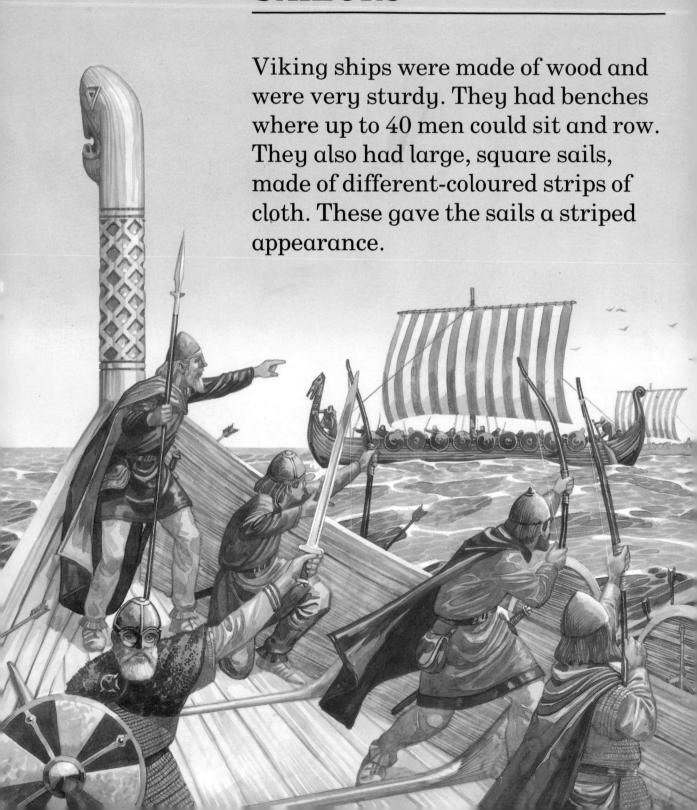

Although the Vikings were very good sailors, they faced many dangers when they travelled by sea. Their small ships often sank in storms, and they fought many sea battles with enemies who tried to stop them from attacking their shores.

Above *A Viking ship.*

Right *Vikings often made their ships look terrifying by carving the post at the front like a dragon's head.*

ATTACKING FOR PLUNDER AND LAND

Viking raiders scrambled out of their boats and stole gold and silver coins, valuable books and other treasures from nearby churches and homes. Then they rushed back to their boats and got away with their **plunder**.

They often left burning buildings behind them, or the bodies of those who had tried to stop them. All over Europe, terrified **monks** began to pray, 'Save us, Lord, from the Vikings' fury'.

Sometimes, whole armies of Vikings sailed to foreign countries, where they forced the people to give up their land so they could settle there themselves.

VIKING WEAPONS

The Vikings fought with spears, bows and arrows, clubs and axes. Their favourite weapons were swords. These were often a metre long and were given names like 'Snake' and 'Leg-biter'. Magic signs were carved on the handles to make the blades more **deadly**. Some sword blades had a groove or hollow down each side. Some people say that these helped the **victims'** blood to flow more quickly!

Left *The metal head of a Viking spear. It was fitted on to a wooden shaft.*

Below *This is the hilt (or handle) of a Viking sword. It was found in Scotland.*

It took a swordsmith a month to make a really fine sword. Swords were treated like family treasures, and fathers passed them on to their eldest sons.

VIKING BATTLEDRESS

When they went into battle, the Vikings carried shields which measured a metre across. They also tried to protect themselves with helmets and **chain mail**.

Right *A Viking helmet found in Sweden. The thick central bar helped to give it strength.*

Some Viking warriors were known as *berserkers*. These men went completely wild on the battlefield and terrified their enemies. They got their name from the bear-sarks (or bear-skin coats) which they wore instead of chain mail. They did not seem to mind getting slashed by their enemies' swords.

VIKING FORTS

The Vikings built forts to keep their armies safe from attack. These were surrounded by a round ditch and a mound of earth. Enemies who tried to attack would have to run down into the ditch, then climb the mound, which probably had a fence on top. Viking soldiers could hide behind the fence and defend themselves with arrows and stones.

Most Viking men lived at home. They formed themselves into warrior bands whenever these were needed. However, some men lived in the forts and were probably full-time soldiers.

Above *A Viking decoration.*

Below *The remains of Viking homes.*

VIKING SETTLERS

Many Vikings built homes in the hills when they settled in new countries. Their long, narrow farmhouses were usually made of wood, stone and soil. Most farms had a number of workshops for weaving woollen cloth, baking bread and making clay and metal articles.

Some Vikings settled in towns. There, they made and sold goods such as gold and silver jewellery, wooden cups and leather bottles.

As well as selling goods locally, the Vikings sent them overseas. For example, the Vikings in Norway sent axe-heads and bowls to other Vikings in England and Iceland.

17

PAGAN BELIEFS

The Vikings were **pagans**. Their gods included Odin, Thor and Freyr, and they prayed to these gods for healthy crops and success in battle. They also **sacrificed** animals as a way of pleasing the gods and gaining their help.

Vikings sacrificing a bull during a pagan ritual.

The Vikings usually worshipped their gods at lonely spots in the open air, but they also built **temples**. Near one of their temples in Sweden, there was a tree where they hung the animals they had sacrificed.

After many years, the Vikings gave up their pagan ideas and became **Christians**.

PLEASURES AND PASTIMES

The Vikings enjoyed many pleasures and pastimes. They played all sorts of musical instruments, including whistles made from sticks or birds' bones. They also liked board games and outdoor activities. They held

Above *This chessman shows the Vikings' skill in carving walrus ivory.*

Right *This carved stone from Sweden shows a man in Valhalla (the place where warriors were thought to go if they died in battle).*

20

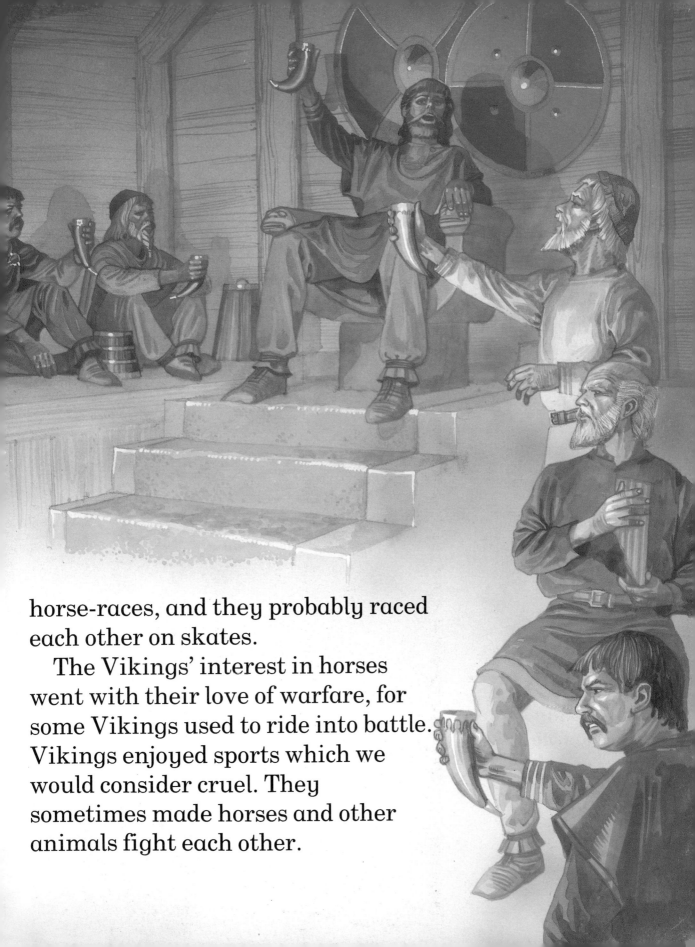

horse-races, and they probably raced each other on skates.

The Vikings' interest in horses went with their love of warfare, for some Vikings used to ride into battle. Vikings enjoyed sports which we would consider cruel. They sometimes made horses and other animals fight each other.

GLOSSARY

Chain mail Light armour made from metal rings that were sewn together.

Christians Followers of Jesus.

Deadly Able to kill.

Monks Men who live in monasteries and spend much of their time praying.

Pagans People who believe in many gods.

Plunder Goods that are stolen on raids.

Sacrificed Killed to please the gods.

Scandinavia Norway, Sweden and Denmark.

Temples Buildings where people worship.

Victims People who are injured or killed.

Walrus Large sea animals with tusks.

BOOKS TO READ

A Viking Sailor by Christopher Gibb (Wayland, 1986).

A Viking Settler by Giovanni Caselli (Macdonald, 1986).

The Vikings by Terence Richard (Wayland, 1986).

Viking Britain by Tony D. Triggs (Wayland, 1989).

Viking Raiders by A. Civardi and J. Graham-Campbell (Usborne, 1987).

INDEX

Picture acknowledgements

The publishers would like to thank the following for providing the photographs in this book: Michael Holford 20 (top and bottom); Ronald Sheridan 11 (right), 16 (top and bottom); Werner Forman 7 (top and bottom), 11 (left), 12 (bottom).

VIKING WARRIORS

Tony D. Triggs

Illustrated by John James

BEGINNING HISTORY

The Age of Exploration
The American West
Crusaders
Egyptian Farmers
Egyptian Pyramids
Family Life in World War II
Greek Cities
The Gunpowder Plot
Medieval Markets
Norman Castles

Plague and Fire
Roman Cities
Roman Soldiers
Saxon Villages
Tudor Sailors
Tudor Towns
Victorian Children
Victorian Factory Workers
Viking Explorers
Viking Warriors

All words that appear in **bold** are explained in the glossary on page 22.

Series Editor: Rosemary Ashley
Book Editor: James Kerr
Designer: Helen White

First published in 1990 by Wayland (Publishers) Limited
61 Western Road, Hove, East Sussex, BN3 1JD.

© Copyright 1990 Wayland (Publishers) Limited

British Library Cataloguing in Publication Data
Triggs, Tony D.
Viking warriors
1. Vikings
I. Title   II. Series
948'.02

HARDBACK ISBN 1–85210–907–6

PAPERBACK ISBN 0–7502–0920–8

Typeset by Kalligraphic Design, Horley, Surrey.
Printed in Italy by G. Canale & C.S.p.A., Turin.
Bound in Belgium by Casterman, S.A.